FINALISTS

Rae Armantrout

FINALISTS

Wesleyan University Press

Middletown, Connecticut

Wesleyan University Press
Middletown CT 06459
www.wesleyan.edu/wespress
2022 © Rae Armantrout
Manufactured in the United States of America
Designed by Mindy Basinger Hill
Typeset in Adobe Caslon Pro

Library of Congress Cataloging-in-Publication Data
available upon request

Hardcover ISBN: 978-0-8195-8067-2
Paperback ISBN: 978-0-8195-8068-9
Ebook ISBN: 978-0-8195-8069-6

5 4 3 2 1

FOR RON SILLIMAN

—

my first reader

Contents

FINALISTS

THREAT LANDSCAPE

Hang On

Domestic as
an empty shopping cart
parked on a ledge
above a freeway.

—

Artifactual as
an acorn barnacle.

"What is the purpose of barnacles?"
people ask the internet.

Barnacles are filter feeders.

They're fish tank décor.

A plaque of barnacles
on top of a toilet—

this cluster
of brittle puckers,

clinging
to its old idea,

these craters striped
pale lavender

for some
unlikely eye.

Red Sky at Night

If the sun rests in the notch
on that mountain ridge.

≈

If an old woman is scribbling.

≈

If an old man alone
in the breakfast room

at the Vagabond Executive
Motor Inn

doing crossword puzzles
beneath *The Early Show*
babble

continues.

≈

If the tree blooms pink
there will be more

than we can imagine
always,

extra promptings
of pure nothing

which we can neither
keep nor forget.

Vultures

1

A product can be authentic;
an object cannot.

This presents a problem.

An identity can be authentic;
an experience cannot.

"How was your sleep experience,"
asks Marriott.

Praise or blame
is the only legitimate response.

2

Vultures wheel over Miami.

A sign that appears
day after day
is not a sign.

The library boasts a fine collection
of books written in private
languages.

3

Identity is made
of select experiences.

4

When you are genuinely sick,
the leaves recede

and the flickering holes between them
come forward—

not angels, but
unnamed objects

Who's Who

Yeats saw a fish
as a mysterious girl

which made the world seem
more fuckable.

He wanted to follow her
home
after he killed her,

but, of course, did not.

2

"Here's the thing,"
says the brand spokesmodel

waving her Diet Coke

and sounding beleaguered
yet defiant,

"just do *you*"

Contrast

What's to like
if not contrast?

Shadows beneath
the model's sharp

cheekbones, her ample
yet precise lips.

Clean lines separating
bounty
from its opposite.

This is not
what I want

to want.

These eyes
on the hypothetical

distance.

Array

A human begins
by claiming

to be something else:

a red bird
in a picture book;

a little red
Corvette.

This is known as capture
or entrainment.

How will she split
the differences?

A stream system
seen from above;

tuning fork twigs
in winter forests.

Threat Landscape

1

Life began with general irritability,

then developed lateral suppression,

the ability to boost some signals
while tamping others down—

attention—

creating a high contrast world
with exaggerated peaks and troughs,

the threat landscape,

projected now on screens
by paid experts.

2

You're right, Sasha.
I forgot

The butterflies are frightening

with their abrupt approaches
and batty swerves.

They mix the outside in.

You're right.
We don't know what will happen.

Visible from Space

In the crosswalk, a woman plods,
swinging her arms briskly.

One of many
who act out

the act

they are actually
performing.

While crop circles
parody
the desire to be seen

and I shove off
to look askance.

Doubt
is an out
of body experience.

Instruction

Were you surprised to learn
that you could swap
an "i" for an eye,
and "a" for an apple?"

That's the lure.

Later, you may
want to pray.

—

You may be left
to think your way
from moment to moment

without being told
what a moment is,

if it's something solid.

—

The mad hear language
speak itself
and are humble before it.

They receive instruction.

—

The child in her crib
turns her head restlessly,
says, "aaah, aaah"
like an engine left running.

Ceremonial

They change arsenate
to arsenite
and back. They
pant.

‗

To capitulate
is to give in;

to recapitulate
is to repeat
in brief.

‗

Fuchsia shadow;
dangling beads.

This
is *my*
body,

    which

‗

They pass one
atom
between them:

"Take and eat."

Provisions

To suck dry.

To mean anything
       by.

By itself, each breath
is a sample.

I come in, decide
what's missing.

Ions,
a concentration gradient,
and a means of transcription

just to scratch the surface.

Just to get ahead
of myself

I will need a special
proboscis.

Findings

A Gift from the Universe:
This message has no content.

—

In this animation someone
has personified the synapses.

—

A raindrop,
pendulous,
at the end
of a long twig,

I

have great respect
for the recalcitrance
of objects.

The Music

"Costume jewelry"
is what we once called this
elaborate pendant
of glass beads

on the middle-aged blonde
leaning against the Safeway
smoking angrily

three feet
from a fleshy woman
in fetal position
on the concrete

where two small girls
walk backwards
shoulder to shoulder
squealing.

≈

By pulsing,
bars of music

make as if
to reconsider

First Thought

1

It was no accident
sight rhymed with light,

they thought.
Mistaken identity

begat fear
and love.

Then a dark boulder
stood up

in the shape
of a large dog

or else it was smooth
and dry, cool

to the touch.

2

Each pitching frond
so much

and so little

like the arched neck
of a horse

tossing its
headless head.

System Processing

1

In the new view, a system is conscious
when the information within it
is both differentiated into parts
and integrated as a whole.

—

At the estate sale, every room is filled
with a different kind of doll—
Barbies, babies, Raggedy Anns—
side by side
on beds, chairs, counters.

2

        Contrails,
sun on power lines—

slant rhyme—

member with membrane,
number with numb.

3

To get an idea
is to place one thing

beside another,
see how they look,

whether they're a good fit—
though I don't want them

to fuse.

I know I will want
to move them again.

My Place

1

I probably think this world
is about me.

How I carry myself:

warm yellow
        furnace
on the horizon,

two upturned wisps,
almost mocking,
in the upper right.

Ripples exhaust themselves
on gravel.

My reflections
caught
in a rock pool.

2

"Black ops, black sites," sung
with a Beach Boys lilt.

Irony is displacement
and who doesn't
feel displaced?

It's hard to locate
the ache
in the swarm.

"From a call center perspective"

Circles

1

First they told me
the future would solve
the present.

Then they told me
the present
would solve the future.

The present is the world
minus intention.

I'm not allowed there.
They know this.

I begin a string
of letters, picketing
distance.

2

The Cheerios
in the babies' cups
are full of Roundup.

"Circle,"
one girl chirps.

The Sleep Problem

1

"If there's anything I can do
to help me," I said.

That's not what I meant.

I must hold my intention
in my mind's eye
or it will go astray.

I must remember
to intend
to hold it
tenderly.

2

"Kickity-doodah," I say,
when you flop over
in bed, thrashing—

meaning zippity-brouhaha
in a language I keep forgetting
you don't speak.

3

A sentence
begins and ends

in the present
but on the way

we need to hurry.
Zippity-Doo-Dah

is a slave song
commissioned by Walt Disney.

Elmer Fudd aims
his blunderbuss,

his boundless, abstract
rage.

Twinge

It's true, dreams
have no meaning;
dreams are meaning—
morsels of it.

Nothing
has itself.

≡

As I recall,
someone provisional
died and we were all
sad for a bit. Twinge.

I wore a T-shirt
with a tiger on it. Questionable
taste, I knew. Like a joke,
it almost meant something.

And I knew of what
looked like a bomb
in a bag on a bus
in passing.

It was my dream,
but I was in it
with the rest. I was
one of them.

which is fine

Startle Reflex

I

Ford's robodogs
roam the factory floor
and enjoy a good
belly rub.

≈

People are startled to discover
that their inner monologues
are ghostwritten.

≈

A sentence that once made sense
and now does not
appears haunted.

≈

Experts are surprised to learn
sparrows across North America
have changed their tune.

≈

"Let's just make it to the end."

2

Everyone's riveted
by the shock

of the disaster victims,

the way they search
for words.

Sutra

My sylph,

silver snakeskin
grid drifting
with the current.

I wish!

=

An object
of reflexive action.

It means to go
around again.

=

One crow barking
frantically
as a small dog
left in an apartment.

=

Practice self-hypnosis.

The Pacific trash vortex.

The Test

Do you ever get bored while urinating?

Are your dreams full of impassioned speeches which later appear
nonsensical?

Do you recognize the speakers?

Do you feel they are making a fool of you?

What is the true meaning of the word fool?

Is a wind blowing from heaven?

Do you believe your dreams are previews of the afterlife or world
to come?

When you hear someone express a thought which you have
also entertained, does this make you feel a) reassured, b) bored or
c) threatened?

Do you enjoy reflections? If so, did your mother mimic your facial
expressions when you were an infant?

Do floor lamps reflected in windowpanes
resemble distant settlements?

Have you been pre-approved?

As It Happens

"I like purple," she said, and her elders gave her
many purple doodads.

Then her sister said, "I like blue," and, by good luck,
the same thing happened.

Now everything blue belongs to Sasha,
while everything purple belongs to Renee.

This system is often self-monitored, but
sometimes conflict occurs.

What to do in the case of lavender?

≡

Math will only answer
whether two terms are equal.

This one is an owl
or skull

and this is a butterfly
or else

some bright stitches in fabric.

Dimensions

Think of

a cowboy hat
on a bobblehead
AI
atop the dash
of an electric car
in China

as depth.

Then length
is the difference

between these bare ribs
of cloud

and your white hair
somewhere

in the scrum.

How to Disappear

1

You had been swinging restlessly
between the appearance of spontaneity
and the appearance of serious thought.

You had been changing lanes
after a glance
in a mirror honest about
its tendency to distort.

What choice did you have?

It was soothing to watch
wisps of smoke
from a nearby chimney
disappearing
one by one.

2

Do you like pulses,

ridges, ripples
stretching into obscurity?

Would you prefer a flicker
to a steady light source?

This one stutters
slightly,

hesitant,

as if it could hold something
in reserve

Much

To know someone is to know what they think
they're doing.

"What do you think you're doing?"

is not a question to be asked
of an animal or plant.

Understanding this question
is what makes us human!

That was one idea I had.

Pretend play develops in babies
between eighteen and twenty-four months.

They are preparing their answers.

—

I just wanted to get
an impression,

and then to make an impression
on you. Though I don't care

much for you. Don't
leave me alone

with these notions.

The Fold

"Let us," he said
"make man,"

as if he had to ask
someone's permission

even if always
only

his own.

≈

To practice is to repeat
what has not yet
occurred.

≈

We get signals
from the future.

We're invited to grow
by entwining,

twinning.

Being duplicitous?

≈

A rose by any other
rose

is its own
paradise

of luminous
folds

Ready

It is always possible.

There are several forms
it is more or less
likely to take

at any point—
but it *won't*
except by chance.

I need you
to locate this,
get at it

where it almost
is, almost isn't
floating in near vacuum.

Feel it out
until "ping"
is its pronoun.

I am ready
to be displaced.

Late Remarks

There's not much I can say.

We're all going to die.
That didn't come out right.

"I'm doomed," is so melodramatic.
"I'm so doomed" is cutesy.

"I'm in trouble"
sounds like a confession
on an old-time cop show.

"We're in trouble now," sounds like
we're about to be sent
to the vice-principal—

that loser!

He'd never understand.

Ghost World

Memories are ghosts
of people not yet dead.

Everyone believes in them
(believes them).

When they disappear,
they let the cold in.

≈

In the cold, things
come closer
without moving,

becoming more and more
distinct.

It's not possible to touch them.

≈

The conjunctions are frozen;
the hinges:

"now."

≈

Now tiny birds
are bouncing

through the corpse
of the wisteria.

not as yet

The News

We wanted to tell someone everything

(or everyone something)—

how large and limp

the leaves were

in the half-sun,

but what is "half-sun"

finally?

—

We'd been "relaxing

protections"

in our sleep again,

it seemed.

Now we were fewer.

—

Some imagined St. Peter
as a special concierge

or a supercomputer
listening—

did he listen?—

to what he must
already know,

hearing only
ones and zeroes,

plusses and minuses.

=

Was that at least something?

=

Over and over,

first one tall stalk

and then its twin

dips westward

and recovers

That's my story
and I'm sticking with it.

Surprise, Surprise

It began
with sensing difference,

but since mind
is the gape
of surprise
propped open,

we can stop
and think.

If comparisons are sketchy,
what about contrasts?

≈

Since mind
is the gape of surprise
propped open,

we get bored.
What's the good of that?

≈

Since mind is the gape
of surprise propped open,

a rollercoaster
has been placed
between those painted lips.

≈

I keep rolling
this lozenge
around on my tongue.

Where's the good in it?

Blues

Why is there careful language

instead of nothing
to be said?

Look!

By kicking the table
I make the light
blue ring

in the dark
blue water

in the blue plastic bottle
shudder

and cause a white bolt
to flicker

across the surface
of the coffee.

I tweak the illusion
before me

best.

Self-Composure

Every eight or nine minutes, I check
to see that enough time has passed.

I am accurate as a frog
hopping between lily pads.

Though I have no sense of
what I've skipped over
or why I came down
where I did.

At the dream conference,
I go down a plastic slide
on cue, shouting the word
"enjoyment."

In my defense, I have
my doubts.

In relaxation videos,
the stars steadily converge
on a cosmic horizon
while the observer
stays put.

I am one of several,
perched alone
at these blond tables,
where the supermarket
joins Starbucks.

Destinations

"You want nuggets; you got nuggets. Here!
You gonna *not* eat nuggets after I bought them?
You're gonna just eat Cheetos," she snaps,
"when we're almost to our destination?"

Yes, she said "destination."

What story follows them where they're headed?

Alone at another table, a man who, like the kids,
holds a bag of Cheetos, cackles and coughs

Where does he fit in?

"Oh, I dropped my candies," he says,
in a high-pitched tone, as if imitating,
maybe mocking, a child's voice.

Vigil

While ripples are shrugged off
the edges

of puddles
and vanish

like that,

with its swollen
knuckle over knuckle,

bamboo
is an abacus—

a tool for counting
to the present.

We're equally vigilant.

We scroll pages
as if scanning thickets

on a long trek
through a dream.

Your Turn

We missed you so much that you came back.

How often does that happen?

Depends on what is meant
by "you."

Maybe never,
maybe every year.

We get confused.

When a new leaf comes out,
what has it come through?

＝

Soon you had added
an "ie" or "a"

or even an "ette"
to your names

because you knew
identity is complicated.

After all, limbs
branch,

hard knots
sprout delicate fans.

Things go sideways.
Vines curl.

＝

When you came back,
you didn't know us,

but you knew your business
and you went to work.

For

This tree is a paradise
of glass and plastic
icicles, raindrops

lit by winking (ticking)
stars.

Stay here.

Red is for ripe
and green for forest.

Now green is for go
and red is for stop.

Blue is for cold
and for heaven above.

"Live for," they say.

Who does?

Familiar Ground

"Eat, Bunny, please.
Sit up and eat."

The child is the mother
and the bunny is the child,
but no one is the cloth rabbit

or Holy Ghost.

≈

To be conscious is to go
through the motions

that have recently been made—
but which?

≈

Angular motion
inscribes an ellipse,

while light runs straight
from imagined
from point to point

Shush

1

A smart pop song
can convince a desperate person
to see herself
as a thrill seeker.

This is considered a job skill.

"Take me to the job.
I'm ready for anything
because I love the adrenaline . . ."

She's a daredevil
or a white devil
on her way to work.

She can beat the rhythm out
on her thighs. I do,

though I have no place to go.

2

Half-formed
letters lean in

to the near silence.

If by write
you mean set down,

shush

of wheels
on wet pavement.

matter
of indifference

Fashion

People are talking about
new hot spots,
viral loads,

Murder hornets,
Crypto currencies.

People are talking about
learning new hobbies,

trying to unlearn
object permanence.

—

A girl's lugging
a toy ambulance
almost too large
for her to lift—

siren ignored in the distance.

—

Clothed in torn cloud scraps,
all innocence,

dressed in dust-ups,
agitated snippets.

Bonsai dissonance—
what we used to call ironic.

"Who told you
you were naked?"

Whistle

The Empire Builder rolls through,
its "whistle" a groan.

A scream is rounded out
in poems, given
a smooth finish.

"Respect the drink!"

In how many recent films
does the hero get his power
from venom,
radiation, or exposure
to chemicals?

How many have been made to host
a hostile symbiont
against their will?

These are moments
that can be flipped, dropped
into 4chan.

By naming its vape flavor
"Unicorn Poop," Drip Star
parodies marketing,

thus appealing
to children.

Siphon

Upwelling—willingly,
unwillingly, the bay's
beautiful wrinkled skin
slate blue

—

What do I have in mind
for my next thought?

—

I'll get attached
to an impression.

It takes the form
of blown glass,

a potbelly
with two siphons,

drawing seawater in
and out.

Functional bubble!

Perfectly transparent,
perfectly opaque.

Curses

I

The old ones thought they could trade
ears of corn

for long life
and happy children.

Can you believe it?

I mean,
do you think it's true?

Can one thing replace another

the way the moon hides the sun
during an eclipse?

2

Imagine there's a person
just like you

beside you
or *besides* you.

If there are two chairs,
you will want the same one.

You will always want it
more than happiness or love.

When you wake up,
you will remember nothing of this.

3

Don't forget,

Mother's hidden under
God whose name

must not be said.

Keep her down there.
She'll be needy,

screeching
after so long

Conjugations

Declarative pointing precedes language.

We're joined here
at the bear
in the Santa suit,

the black-capped chickadee,

the beaded cottage
with no way in
or out.

See?

You press
a stuffed frog
to a stuffed pig
and look up.

"Are they kissing?"
"Are they fighting?"
we ask,

jumping to our old conclusions.

Incognito Mode

This
morning stillness with its
occasional ripples, shivers,
shrugs—

seemingly unprovoked

—

If matter is tufted
energy, then energy

is what?

—

I ask because,
if I know anything,

it's that each thing
is something else.

Transfer

For Mark Kruse

Now they tell us
"orbit" is wrong.

Electrons don't actually
"orbit a nucleus."

Perhaps they are looking for the word
"haunt."

One meaning of haunt
is to frequent.

To be known
to appear.

They say electrons leap
from nonexistent
rung to rung,

giving off energy

as a ghost may vanish
from one room
to materialize in the next,

causing the audience
to jump.

Catch

Over eons, consciousness
developed as a ride-along.

Eyewitness testimony
has been thoroughly discredited

=

Black fir branches feathery
on dusk's blanched
sky—a drawn
breath.

And the acrobatic bats

The Wound

Wherever there is a wound,
a wound is at the center.

Should the reverse
also be true?

Is each center
a sort of wound?

—

A toddler points
to her belly button
and asks, "More?"

More?

—

At the start, we discovered
the meanings
of the sounds we made

and the thunder
yelled "No!"

Phantoms

If metaphors ran backwards,
so that necklaces
were raindrops
on bare twigs,

how much power
could be generated?

2

Proprioception
burns in hell
with no reference points.

3

Sting of sun
on power lines
strung taut
between houses.

This world
made of phantom limbs.

this page is not responding

On Growth

Dressed all in plastic,
which means oil,

we're bright-eyed, scrambling
for the colored cubes

spilled
on the rug's polymer.

Inside each
is a tiny car.

When we can't unscrew the tops
we cry for help.

We're optimists.

⸗

To sleep is to fall
into belief.

Airing even
our worst suspicions
may be pleasurable;

we are carried,
buoyed.

In sleep,
the body can heal itself,
grow larger.

Creatures that never wake
can sprout a whole new
limb,

a tail.

This may be wrong.

Asterisk

Cresting the fence, each leaf
sharply particular, edgy, nearly
identical to its kin.

≈

String of periods.

String of period
living rooms, lights
coming on in them.

≈

One's coordinates

or the coordinates
one is?

≈

To be found
wanting.

≈

How many billion
suns blazing
and the universe
still dark

As If

Time is now divisible to the hundred billionth
of a second.

Such refinement is necessary
in order to order
the volume of exchanges
scrambling
to compose the past.

It seems I crush an ant
and deposit his carcass
on the torn plastic wrap
inscribed, "This bar
saves lives."

But then all thought
is afterthought.

—

But what's a second
if not a pause,

I say,

as if swallowtails
batted summer away,

as if shadows
and their trailing lights
explored the blue couch
uselessly.

Cathexis

When we say the world is haunted
we mean untranslated

               as yet.

A "cathexis"
is a catch basin
in English.

A result of draining
"here" off into "there."

Starbucks' billion plastic straws
are green.

I know the leaves are whispering.

Tell me what my mother meant!

Recent Thinking

Some say the fact that the world is computable
is evidence we're living in a simulation.

And the fact that the simulations *we* create
are improving rapidly is further evidence of this.

It is reasonable to think that any simulation *might*
have been created by one more advanced than itself,

a potentially infinite regress in which
the word "simulation" becomes meaningless.

Experience suggests that simulations are games
with both player and non-player characters.

No character has explicitly stated
that we should destroy the biosphere
to test the limits of the game.

Innovations

The first idea
was to continue.

Hurtling?

But a thought
is a kind of stop.

‗

To continue
is to start over.

‗

The first innovation
was serial

survival.
Is that for real?

‗

Is it clear that
a billion
spruce needles
are good

while a billion green
detergent pods
are not?

‗

"I'm so done! LOL"
say the young,

correctly.

Scare quotes have morphed
into emojis.

Spurge

Here the windows offer nothing
in the way of temporary death,

no metaphors
for old age
to be followed soon enough

by youth.
No secret formula.
Here everything is patent.

If there's a lesson,
it's to do
with eternity's hodgepodge

and the limits
of thought.
Who would think up

the muscular tongues
of the what's-it,
fuzzy and gray-green

next to the rattling
vertebrae
of fronds,

or that euphorbia
(good form?),

formerly known
as spurge.

Flocks

As thoughts take pleasure
in forming,
then break and
retreat.

—

As flocks of crows sweep
low above winter trees
at dusk.

—

As one and one
are one.

On Balance

How a child's excitement
over all new things

is meaning
hovering jerkily above

a word, not settling.

＝

A small girl
shifts a skillet
from one burner
to the next
on a play stove,

laughing.

＝

Goal tracking?

Security exchange?

＝

The way two small flocks,
darting north and south
at once,
clear a marsh path,

make peace.

If you can believe it

—

It may be
anyone's eyes,
enlarged,
look sad.

which is fire

In Reality

Our world is made of particles with names like the Seven Dwarfs:
Strange, Up, Down, Charm, Muon, Gluon, and Tau.

Particles are freaks
of measurement.

In reality, nothing
is waving.

Aloha: hello, goodbye.

Names like the seven
deadly sins.

On the horizon, a large plane's
dawdling.

Let It Go

I

"Let it go," they say, meaning whatever you were just feeling.
And the feeling before that too, if you can recall it. I don't really distinguish
between feelings and thoughts.

When I write I am trying to recapture the shape of a thought,
though I don't believe in ghosts.

When they say "let it go," they may mean you should focus
on what is now before your eyes—
the growing pile of papers
on the desk, for instance, atop which
a plastic bag of colorful rubber bands
has perched.

2

As sleep comes,
I'm often surprised to feel
something give way

or let go,
something I didn't know I was holding—
being held by.

When I die, will this feeling recur?
Will it seem like I'm meeting
someone I know?

Elsewhere

Beauty again
presents itself

as if
for the first time.

It begins, "When I
look up"

and goes on
"the wet eucalyptus

is tossing, twinkling
like the sea."

It puts words in our mouths.
Similes.

Displaced,
it returns.

It can appear
in human form,

but is most often
elsewhere.

Those paired
circles of light,

winking
from the shady branch.

What Follows

It's a good thing

mind's distributed.

"It wasn't me,"

one says,

repeatedly,

"I haven't died."

＝

Each tract,

thus bracketed,

waits

for what precedes,

what follows.

＝

I accept defeat.

To accept defeat
is to regress,

to go back
where you came from.

This may be
the fountain of youth!

I claim it
for myself.

The End

Aspirational love
flickered between them
at the end.

The End.

Some might say
it was conventional
love, but
it was aspirational too.

It got in
all the newspapers.

Don't be a cynic.

≈

Want to hear a different story?

All the insect helpers
were gone in an instant,

the worms
that made the beds,

the moths that worked on
Cinderella's dress.

"Where *are* you?"
intoned the baby girl,

holding both palms up
in the gesture we use

to make light of
our ignorance.

What an excellent mimic!

The Steps

1

I take a step back
and it's like dancing.

But what would it mean
to "return to my roots"?

Is that what the flowers do
in September?

2

Kids make money
and love
by being themselves
on YouTube.

"It only works
if it's authentic."

Was it better
when enthusiasms
had objects—

such as distant wars
or tulips?

Now we pay attention
to attention.

Take a step back
and it's like dancing.

What would it mean
for attention to be empty

like a phrase
repeated too often?

Pursuits

1

What was I just thinking,
I think,
frantic as if
I had lost my key.

Oh, that you'll soon turn away,
toward your cohort,
last door slamming.

2

The difference between the recent dead
whose mention makes us shudder
even if we knew them only
by name
and the long dead
for whom we feel nothing.

3

To be at peace,
picture the missing
supple, silver,
countless
in a distant sea.

Dusk

Not the brass
doorknob

but the reflection
at its center

is my most
private part.

It partakes
of the next

world
and the next

in which I stand
with someone,

fondly mistaking
planes for stars.

Everything

Everything reminds us of sex
the way sex
reminds us of everything

it's not.
An apricot perhaps.

Or the sunset's bridesmaid
chiffon.

All fricatives.

The dimpled, grassy hills
west of the San Joaquin.

The way nothing
is quite

true

and everything bears
repeating

Real Life

A dreamer never wonders
what she will do
after her dream.

A dream can be banal, repetitive
and still be totally engrossing.

This is not to say
it seems *real*.

A dreamer holds no such belief.

The dream's POV
may or may not
be lodged in an image.

These avatars, when they do appear,
are discontinuous,
clearly unnecessary.

A dream needs only
your attention.

In a dream there is no sleep.

Riddance

OK, we've rendered
the rendition

how often?

What were we trying
to get rid of?

We exposed the homeless
character of desire
to the weather.

Shall we talk
about the weather

worsening four times
faster than expected,

eight times,

until the joy
of pattern recognition
kicks in?

> Until the crest
> of the next ridge
> is what remains
> of division.

Some Things

"Nee Nee" and "Ah Ah,"

you'd heard the word before

and there they were—
two ants,

minuscule and flustered.

You were ecstatic.

—

As if each feeling
was a message

from a god

with his or her
own interests.

—

Glacial erratics.

Tossed off the way
one says,

"When I die"

I didn't mean to fall silent.

Chill

Ta-dum.

I want to make something
out of nothing

then sparkle and chill,
chill and sparkle

like a constellation.

A silver droplet hanging
from the tip
of each split leaf.

A drop
and its odd
diminutive.

FINALISTS

Crescendo

THE LIGHT 1

Three o'clock, about two hours of light left,
glorious on the ornamental pear,
some leaves grizzled dark red.
The large leaves of what we think is
mock orange—yellow again, as when they first
appeared—and will soon fall.

I'll miss you so much when you're gone.
I'd miss you if I looked away
or if a cloud covered the sun.
I miss this moment
as it goes on happening.

THE LIGHT 2

That little tree,
leaves now grizzled
gold and dark
red, is past
all transaction—
stiff in crescendo,
praising no one.

The gold my people
razed the world for—

cashed out there.

Buy In

Yes, we did
ask to be born.

Not all of us, of course,
only the first few.

They must have bought in
to this round robin
duress:

the gasp,

the gnawing hunger,
then the actual gnawing.

Maybe they did it
the way we'd put on

a corset or toe shoes
one night

and feel fabulous.

To be able to repeat themselves
must have seemed

like such a thrill
at first.

But who *were* they
if not that trick—

that breathless
pirouette?

Password

1

As if the problem were
that I couldn't stuff
the bulky text
into the child's backpack
and was late for a class
I never registered for
so long ago!

2

"Business tiptoes
in a world of masks."

"People relate"
to a transparent sham.

As if genre
weren't camo.

3

Strange to wake rested
after these dreams
of disaster and scandal
not registered as such.

4

When I've stared long enough
at the rough skinned,

snub nosed, or
tough nippled

lemons,

I will give attention
to World Password Day.

Lions

Lion taming
exists to make us think
that the ferocity of lions
is fake.

Or lion taming exists
to parody our sense
of human mastery
over the earth.

Of course,
any thought
is a shot in the dark.

But a poem exists
to contain it.

Now a thought
is a watched pot.

Quit

A long flirtation
based on mutual recognition
of the scarcity
of local resources.

> The way you fiddled
> with the buckles
> of my raincoat
> forever,
> glancing up
> to meet my eyes—
> shy and perhaps
> embarrassed.

A private joke
about the lack
of a more general
understanding.

> The way you dropped a crayon
> down your shirt front
> again and again
> laughing raucously—
> best joke ever!

Is this a plausible
vision of heaven?

> Quit being silly!

Parasol

1

"Where are you *going*?"
a three-year-old mock-scolds

snails
climbing walls

so slowly
we can't see them move.

2

Sleek-thorned,
red vine

arm—wayward
artery—

you sport

here
and here

a parasol
of leaves.

Play Fellow

It was like dreaming.

I thought I was carrying animals
to a castle
in a backhoe,

but really I was shoving plastic
down a chute,
no, a hall.

—

Speech is role-playing
before it is thought.

We talk *as if* to others,

then to others,

and then, finally, to ourselves.

—

But really I was speaking
to a roomful of strangers
in words I could almost
make out.

Conditional

I love you
because you said,

"The moon is good
at hiding."

Lonely Girl

It wasn't her fault.

She couldn't have loved
any of them because
they never came out of themselves, emerged
as what?

Disembodied? Transparent?

2

She couldn't explain herself either.

Self is an area
where will intersects
with drift.

It has ruffled, frothy
edges

like a square dance dress.
Look.

3

Lying in the dark,
nose buried in her arm's
crook, she felt like a girl,

or pictured herself as one,

or loved herself as much
as she had
when she was a girl

and first coiled
up. That

was her secret.

Floating

Once there was a woman who told a famous physicist that the universe
rested on turtle backs "all the way down." A perfect anecdote. I don't
think it occurred to him that she might be putting him on. I mean no
disrespect when I say that there's a physicist who claims the universe we
see is made of shrunken universes, small, primordial black holes. That's
what the mysterious "dark matter" is. Naturally, we're in one of these
cosmic pinheads because, "seen from the outside, *our* universe might
look like a black hole." I don't mind. Actually, I like the idea. In each of
these blind spots huge stars are burning, though no one outside can see
them—so the mysterious dark matter is full of obscure light.

Terms of Service

1

The bottom of the ocean
has little to do

with what we mean
by depth:

tangles of explication;
invisible gear

to haul up
synonyms

for what's missing

2

Involuted coastlines
in the supply chain.

Self-assembly
is a hot topic.

A wooden clock
with a bird in it.

Robots that make
personal assistants.

Strange attractors
can explain all day

Greek to Me

1

I don't understand
the word "makeshift,"

but I know how to apply it
to the rickety, wooden
unpainted steps
in front of that house

or to this potted plant—
two hairy, slender
Y-shaped filaments
on a long stalk

like a dousing stick
or a TV aerial.

—

I am told
when I do well.

I almost understand
the word "make-do."

2

You stand
on the plump, strong legs
you don't hate yet.

Stutter

If nothing new comes up,
my last thought
gets stuck—stutters.

Could be a dangling
                    modifier
gone insistent,

ready to fill the world
with itself.
A neat trick.

A hook and eye,
grown exponential.

I prefer snippets
of music
without words,

ripples
on a placid surface—
innocent.

Gone

1

This little begonia
is fierce enough to
matter.

To have a bearing

on.

To press a point

and to be of some

concern.

2

This music gently
shakes itself

as if it had forgotten something.

Then it goes nowhere
urgently.

It settles here and there
to repeat a motif

like a bee
visiting flowers.

It winds concerns
on a spindle.

To hear it
is to have a mother

retrospectively

Context (2)

I resent the wired beads.

That's obscure
as it should be.

Having popped up recklessly,
they (or it) should

stay hidden.

＝

Did I wish
to "come back around"?

"Circles an old woman's
fingers trace
on the nubs of
her chair arms."

I thought circles
were empty;

          now

I'm orbiting
with one finger

while thinking of something
"else."

These Days

TASTE

We've developed a fondness for "mid-century murk"—meaning the last mid-century, not the one soon to come with its increasingly toxic air. We've developed a taste for the coldest of cold cases being worked by impossibly earnest child sleuths or laconic county sheriffs in tiny desert towns. What is making the phone lines crackle? Does this noise sound menacing to you?

We've developed a necrophiliac's taste for remoteness. Those *just* beyond living memory are the most distant, the strangest of strangers.

TASKS

Each day I stare at the gap between "and" and "then" with the sense that, if I am very quiet, something important will come out of it. Am I languid, pensive, or anxious? Any one of these words is a polaroid I am reluctant to inhabit, yet, taken together, they make a pyramid, that most stable of forms.

SIGNALS

Everything the children do is a reenactment of something half grasped or glimpsed. We call such portrayals "play," but they are similar to the way aliens might attempt to communicate by reproducing signals from old TV broadcasts, including the static between stations.

This one uses a falsetto to indicate that there are two of her, the one speaking now and the one we will never hear.

Plague Year

What we share is the Chicano detective in 1930s Los Angeles
torn between his loyalty to his community
and his loyalty to his partner.

≈

What we have in common is the orphan girl,
trained as an assassin, secretly working
against the cabal of rogue agents
who plan to make use of her skills.

≈

What we share is distance: telephone poles
leaning this way and that, a wayward
crowd that staggers drunkenly
toward an empty, mauve horizon.

≈

We can't wait to see
who dies next.

On Melancholy

What I thought of as a pleasant lingering
on things,
tender,
without the flurried rush of hope,
Freud called "Melancholia":

"a state in which a person grieves
for a loss she is unable to identify."

What I experienced
as a general attunement,
wishing only to continue—

a suspended attitude—

Freud described as "narcissistic identification with the object
that becomes a substitute for the erotic
cathexis."

And what if, in my case,
there are multiple objects—

whatever appears outside this window—

the dangling threads
of the weeping cypress—

how I would love to make
the elegant, dismissive
gestures
of those long fingers—

beside the white
phone lines, plunging
almost straight down,
or up,
taut,

catching occasional rays of sun,

like a child's idea
of a message

Cheating

1

I want to give you the questions in advance.
This will seem silly, but listen.
There isn't much time.
Everything depends on it.

What is the same?
What is different?

This may be extra hard
for twins.

Which is larger?
Which is more important?

What does the cat in the picture
know?

Is he sad because the frog is gone?

2

As you go on, the questions
will become more challenging.

Do you really love the same
inflatable black cat?

Why that one?

Who loved it first?

Absorption

Once established,
a thing

is a fact,
and a fact

is an item,
an object

of pity.

—

For the yellow slime mold,
on the other hand,

the map *is* the territory,
and the territory

is a body
of pulsing, fractal veins,

inquisitive causeways.

For the slime mold,
the map

is a stomach
and a brain.

Hydrangea Is a Strange Word

Heaven is blue
and purple—

but everyone knows that!

Around the dark
plateau
of stamens,

a ring of simple flat
blue flowers:

a *carousel.*

Sayings

Playing ball across the street,
one boy shouts, "I'm gonna show you
my whole potential!"

"Better do it now,"
the other taunts—

like a clumsy translation
from what?

I'm alone with the sun
in my lap.

"Not a bad day,"
I say to myself,

repeating this
like a bird call.

Heat

Statements appear
                    to step back.

There's a reflection
                    that we should not let

hotheadedness distract us.

There's an echo that we must
consider.

There are things yet
                    to be done:

"Debunk mysteries
from the art world";

"Build your own
magic library."

＝

Blank scraps—

                    day moths—

still sail
on the updrafts.

Too Much Information

Dears,

the backwards-facing S,
a decoration in the iron rail,
was here when I came,
with its extra curlicues
at each end,
and a miniature
version of itself
like a fetus
affixed to its middle.

I'm telling you more, perhaps,
than you need to know.

The sun on the rail's
inner curves
is a private matter,
something like love,
despite the roar
of the nearby freeway.

I mix love up with safety.

2

It's hard to come by good
ideas
while California
goes up in flames.

It's hard to have
a new idea
when temps in LA
rival those in Iran.

I can't say anything
more original than:
"Gender Reveal Party
Sparks Massive Wildfire"
in tinder-dry forest.

3

You never know
what will matter next.

Pack everything.

Lapse

1

To keep my abridgment
consistent
with its previous iterations

and with that of others
is a nearly
all-consuming task,

allowing just a thin trickle
of the new
to be processed—

or so I'm told—

but those whose recaps
self-contradict
hardly seem better informed.

2

When intention stutters,
it is not a pleasant
flicker.

Anyone can be
hypnotized
by blinking lights.

But one can also find
oneself
mesmerized by nothing

while deep inside,
in bones and gut,

the thoughts
think themselves.

In Response

First comes the excitement of mutual alarm,

the bursts of caws
and tweets.

First comes the flurried spread
of scenarios and statistics.

Then boredom. Then?

≈

What account can you give?

I spent all afternoon cracking my neck and watching the
bright cold day dim.

≈

Did Tiny's Wooden Alphabet meet your expectations?

≈

The three-year-old waves her bubble wand, says
"Oh look, a bubble,"
while running to pop it

in the new/old video footage.

How many stars would you give this?

≈

Thousands of returning passengers wait hours
at cramped airport checkpoints
to be asked
if they feel sick.

=

I pop,
            pop
pop

that question.

Or I coalesce
around it

as ice crystals

form around specks
of coal dust

or pollen.

I begin
to self-report.

Think Back

Say an idea is math
without numbers.

For instance, you could say
that an idea
distorts consciousness
as a massive object
distorts space.

Such distortion
is sometimes known
as attraction.

It pulls
a debris field
into orbit

(or a halo of microplastics).

You slip
from one thought
to the next
as a snake
sloughs off old skin.

Thinking back
is less reliable
than you might think.

Second Life

1

I collect words to fill empty space.

"I think a lot of their enduring appeal
is how real it is."

≈

Many people believe
charismatic objects
are spirits.

They think such spirits
can enliven us.

≈

I like to collect smooth
multicolored rocks,

so distinct from the dirt or mud
they rest on,

carry them awhile,
then set them down—

like this.

2

I dreamed I was captioning
the last dream I had—

or one that was playing
simultaneously
elsewhere in my head.

Our Days

In Chuck's dream, a strange woman
is smoking in our kitchen.

She's doing her best, she says,
exhaling into the oven.

Then three military men
burst in without knocking.

They say they've come
to establish order,

but their uniforms are strange.
Chuck suspects they're really salesmen.

Their leader stands too close
as he begins his pitch—

close enough to spread a virus.

2

I take a photo of a house
painted half blue, half pink.

Why am I drawn
to things that make no sense?

Or is their sense excessive?

You need to decontextualize
an object
in order to see it,

I once said.

Last sloth
in a pocket of rain forest;

exquisite scent
of hyacinth

wafted
on the wingless breeze.

Panicle

The hope is that the fungal
mycelium
exchange messages
through a vast underground network.

The hope is that
we're not alone.

A small black spider
cautiously explores
the wet plastic trash bag.

A woman somewhere
across the street
says, "I don't know,"
and laughs.

The hope is in the facts.

Buzzing, a bee slams
time and again
against a blue-black wall.

The hope is that the universe
is formed
of an infinite number
of Y-shaped prongs,

rocking stiffly in the wind,
spitting out
lilac panicles.

But

We'll stare a long time at water.

It's so much
like the flowing grids
we are.

"But what?"
says the cuckoo bird

within—
precise, repetitive

as if popping
bubble wrap.

Confounding

1

Angel-ologists didn't know what they were talking about, still they were prescient. This often happens. They had no idea they had predicted the behavior of subatomic particles.

The simplicity of angels confounded them. Angels, they reasoned, had no distinctive qualities. And yet millions, billions, perhaps an infinite number were thought to exist. There was a baffling blandness in this excess.

Many believed that angels, like electrons in an atom, could move between two places without passing through the intervening space, which calls the nature of space into question.

Most believed angels, being emanations, had no will of their own, though some had managed to rebel—or at least behave unpredictably.

It was thought that, as with photons, more than one angel could occupy the same space, and that, above all, threw *one* into confusion.

2

There came a time when everyone publicly congratulated themselves for having survived—but perhaps neither congratulation nor survival was to be taken literally. This was clearly no celebration. The mood was dark, even bitter. First there was the issue of what each had survived, which required a lengthy drop-down menu. Then came a list of those absent— about whom, perhaps, the less said the better, as the public and the dead could easily be confused.

*The angel lore in this poem owes a debt to Eliot Weinberger's book *Angels and Saints*.

Which Is Which

Being famous is the top
future goal

in a sample of ten-
through twelve-year-olds.

Being recognized as

having been
seen.

Once I wanted
to be seen

as a famous dead
outlaw.

Then I liked
being called

"incisive,"
"ambiguous"

as a sudden pain.

—

Everyone knows these
small, shrill birds.

No one cares
which is which.

Loose

What I want in a word
is the difference

between the loose petaled
sunset or salmon-colored

rose
and the tightly folded

whorl

of the pale lavender
beside it—

along with their mutual
refusal
of red.

=

Those "water-colored clouds"—

I'm glad I got them
off my chest.

Swarm

The way I call this buzz
of urgent voices
rising,
getting clearer,
a "nap."

=

The way Sasha hears bees
in the butterfly bush
and runs back
squealing,
"I'm a doggy!"

Cloud

As we grow up "simmering plural possibilities" get pared down, says Andrew Miller in a book I haven't read. This reminds me of the probability wave in physics—that dreamy mathematical cloud any subatomic particle *is* before it somehow gets measured. I wonder if lives are probability waves in slow motion.

=

That's the thought I was trying to have while my husband was reading me facts about the pandemic, place names, death tolls. It was bad and getting worse as it had been every day for—how long now?

=

The aging pair in the dream were reliving their past life as a famous/ infamous couple with the aid of their small entourage in an unfurnished beach house. Lackeys broke up reenacted quarrels and smiled wearily at old antics. I was touched. Was I a journalist? A fly on the wall?

=

My husband is repeating the same pandemic statistics in the same raised voice to someone who called. He has shut his office door as if this was a private talk, but he's practically yelling, telling whoever it is the same things he told me. Am I irritated or jealous?

=

I'm not a good audience, I tell myself, but that's not true. I was a great audience member for the people in my dream.

=

If both people and, say, photons, are realized by a process of incalculable loss, then I have discovered a secret identity and will receive a pleasurable throb.

Count

1

The future
is a sweetener

children have to learn
to crave.

2

As cushy clouds
in full sun

are taken
to betoken—

Streaming

1

The ring of the pickaxes
of people searching
for the bones
of their dead relatives
plays in an art museum
in Mexico City

on repeat.

"It's very real for them,
isn't it?"
asks PBS anchor
Jeffrey Brown,
dreamily,
leaning in.

2

Then geese cycle madly
across a pond
like Wile E. Coyote
three feet past the cliff—

catch lift
and join the great migration.

You can too,
they seem to suggest.

Time's arrow is pointed elsewhere.

Not even Looney Tunes
is forever.

3

But if drug gangs,
the mechanics of flight,
and Wile E. Coyote
occur in my mind's eye
in rapid succession,
I need to believe
there's some reason—
or else things fall apart.

Ant trails
and cobwebs
from one thought
to the next,

strings of Xmas lights.

Help

During an accident, time slows down
not when there is still a chance
of averting disaster,
but, rather, when it's too late
and we return
from the flurry
of failed actions
to watch things
as they accrue,
occur

—

If any release of tension
is pleasant,

shouldn't this also
be true of death?

—

The sky sifts downward.

The remaining light
is pendulous.

Clarity is what
the leaves
are spittled with.

"Did you call me?"
"No."

Finalist

Nothing to see here.

Pinecones litter
the gutters.

Whose turn is it
to blow on the mirror,
Mama?

—

Each pushes forward
in her wild eagerness
to take part
in a ritual.

"Is this that thing
about fireflies?"

Maybe.

—

We use similes to show
things are connected—

and they are,
just not in the ways we say.

—

A hole in fresh dirt
surrounded by orange cones
into which
a crow peers,
hops sideways,
then peers again.

=

"These wildlife finalists
will take your breath away"

Influence

At the top of my game
I was paid modestly

to place riddles
about ruination

in the pages
of the glossies

read by thousands,
perhaps hundreds—

to be a twee ghost
some might say—

while suicidal influencers
"blew up"

in the neighborhoods.

Given a Choice

1

See the best of last month.

Take a first-person journey.

Watch an airplane
make a battleship disappear.

Remember the blue and purple flowers
now limp, white, spotted pink.

Scan the surface
for anomalies.

2

We choose music
for the way it bifurcates—

shifting as if
it was moving on,

coming around like

to repeat
was the same as

setting off

Ghosting

Millions of bots
are furious and appalled.
"Dire news," they say.
"Please read."

⹀

Please call
and make my phone ring;

it's lost and you too
are missing.

⹀

Is there a word for this?

When one expects nothing,
no one,

but can still feel

⹀

Anything
can be a ghost—

a second shoe,
a tweet.

One Thing

1

I had a thing
about sensation.

It was small, dedicated,
working its way in

to me.

I was reminded of a bee
burrowing

into the smooth cone
of a flower,

how it wags its bottom
in the air—

funny.

2

I had a thing
about love.

Love was lying
nose to skin.

It was mutual agreement
to a node by node
release

of attention—

an operation
infinite in principle.

Pyramid

I dreamed a family drama—
a kind of pyramid scheme—
three generations of messiahs,
an old man, his son
and a stolen baby
who had to be regularly replaced
in secret.

The son was a wastrel, some
comic relief.

Then the flowers at the window
got bigger, nearer

more engrossing.

That was "all I ever wanted,"
I tried to explain.

Wait for It

1

The EPA ends a ban on perchlorate
in drinking water
after it is shown to cause brain damage
in infants.

The CDC has a plan for the zombie apocalypse.
Zombies eat brains.

I think I've seen this.

2

We fall in love with concepts
such as home or adventure,
glamor or kindness.

We confuse concepts with people.

One woman who loved home and adventure
lived in a small suburban house
with an angry drunk
for forty years.

The Book

1

The poet uses enjambment
so that the reader
has the constant
small pleasure
of thinking, "Oh, that
makes sense,
after all."

⸗

So that the reader
and writer
share mixed feelings—
shame at falling
for this easy trick
and the satisfaction
of catching one's
fall

mid-air,

as one hugs oneself
in bed before
submitting to sleep.

2

God doesn't skim
to get to the good
part. This

is the first mystery
of God.
He is in no hurry

to meet his own
image.

For millennia, he sets
sea scorpion
against scorpion,

swiveling
in their clunky armor,
brandishing their erect
tails.

Forever is nothing.

When he does see someone
looking back,
he screams

"Stop imitating me!"

What Counts

First breath, best breath.
I don't mean anything by that.

Shale over shale.
I concentrate on acts

to keep from repeating
words in my head.

I sit up and copy them
in bed.

"So, so glad
I'm not doing that.

So glad I'm not
the one doing that."

These waves slide over
gray shingled sand.

One covers another
as the first draws back.

Best breath, first breath

Fanfic

Medicine is "emasculated"
by statistics,
says Senator Paul.

━

Replacement Robin
will be destroyed
by Original Robin
unless Replacement Batman
(Dick Smith)
is willing to step in.

━

"As for we who love to be astonished,"

to attract a female
the lyrebird
mimics a chain saw.

Self-Talk

A child "self-talks"
inside scare quotes.

How does that happen?

—

"Our popular classic
experiences
are back!"

—

She names what she's doing
as she does it.

She swaddles herself
in the soothing gauze
of words.

—

Now, almost invisible,
she'll pose.

—

"Look back
at your memories
from this day."

—

(Assume the middle
distance—the best place
for someone else to stand.)

Talking Points

Processing plant blames
living conditions.

—

Incredulity
mimics boredom.

—

Children prefer to listen
to a talking animal.

This tells us something
about the world,

but what?

—

There is thought
at work here,

but it's not traceable

to a known speaker
or agent.

—

"I'm Tiger, Tigger, Trigger,"
says the sock puppet.

The Door

For Robert and Jess

1

Again the endless
brief cascade
of white wisteria
against that wall

as if "all along
there's been a sweet
marriage" taking place.

2

I work at thought
curation.

I don't pretend this is a cure.

I merely hint
that there's a secret door
connecting those two rooms.

For our purposes,
it doesn't matter

whether this is true.

Poem

The blueberry at the end
of the largest of three
clear plastic compartments
is

"There, there," you think
to say.

I mean I do.

Alone in the smeared plastic
on the glass coffee table,

the berry is so
sweet and so cold—

its cup not yet
on the way to a landfill,
followed by seagulls.

Visualization

Check the box
with a pen rummaged

from an orange, pleated
faux-leather purse—

a clutch bag
to be exact—

two brass knobs on top
twisted shut

like a woman's legs.

Like what??

If that's my mind,
I don't want it!

Guided Meditation

Picture small fish nibbling
at your aches and pains—

tasty morsels!

≈

Imagine moments replicating
several hazy trees.

Imagine there are no such things
as moments.

≈

As birds skip
in paired flight
like school kids,

your pulse flutters.

Pow

If a blow can lead
to seeing stars,

the universe explodes.

The old cartoonists
knew this.

"Yow!"
exclaims the star-jasmine.

Now it's now.

Backyards are full
of rat-a-tat.

The birds ask
to insert this

short sequence
of code.

The Mysteries

When seen from a certain angle,
she is "mysterious and dark."
You love that about her.

Angle or distance?

—

Or you've got her number.

She's a nihilist,
an exhibitionist,

a tad precious,
pointlessly fastidious,

hermetic, cold.

—

People are obvious
until you love them.

Then they're black boxes,
deep-sixed flight recorders,
or presents that won't open.

This is why
the word "why"
so often sounds
like an accusation.

Tell It to the Judge

I admit I skipped
"Sixteen Relatable Moments"

When the flurry of wind-chimes stops
I listen.

I write, "Closing dimples
                        of sweetness."

When another human speaks,
I turn away.

—

I admit I confuse
eternity
with equivocation—

and that I do it on purpose,
as the leaves

nod and shake.

Bingo

Madly petaled, these
mock-orange flowers,
tattered as the little
passing clouds,
will soon fall.

⎯

A child plays matching games,
placing
the image of a cardinal
on the image of a cardinal.

Your Attention

We ask you to pay attention,

by which we mean direct it
as if you existed
apart from it.

This must sound like hocus-pocus,
but we assure you
it is very real.

An afterimage
can control the future.

We don't have time
to be more specific.

I don't have time to sit here
or there.

I don't have time to save
this document.

I don't have time to continue
reading
about spider cognition.

Spiders who "actively promote
signal transmission throughout the web,"

who "outsource information processing
to environmental features,"

"eliminating the need
for an internal model"

or soul.

Fond

1

The feeling in my eyelids
closer to tension
than pain, closer
to exasperation than
tension.

They told us the right word
would open any door.

Woke up with the words
to "Little Surfer Girl"
running through my head—

not a fantasy of freedom
I was ever
really fond of.

2

Patches of smooth water
carried downstream
amid cross-current
ripples—

I want to say "intact"—
as if
I might be
one of those
blank
        ovals.

Wishes

True or false:
it's easy
to imagine
being someone else.

—

What about the sleek crows
strutting on the lawn?

Are they ever uncertain?

—

"I don't want anything,"
the child says mournfully
when we ask her
to make a wish.

She can see *we* want
something,
but she can't tell what.

Meeting

In physics, every moment
lasts forever,

if seen from
increasing distance.

In none does
my mother
meet her grandchildren.

=

In your dreams, your space
is occupied by strangers;

in mine I'm with you
in an unrecognizable place.

=

Or I'm out and need to reach you,
but must press my fingers just so
into the small pillow
people call a phone.

The

Let Scott equal "I."

Scott says, "I
asked my team
to pull your records."

I am regularly updated.

I think of one thing,
then another—

a monarch then a butterfly—

now the two are comparable.

I speak of the past
and the future.

Scott is Scott-free
by nature.

I can be removed
from the equation,

leaving this blinking cursor,
"the"

While

The accumulated brilliance of fall

The leaves holding that brassy high note as long

The almost tender flickers
from the trees, the wires, the bottle
left out on a ledge

signal that we're all
in this together—

while "this"
is a passing impulse
traveling through the air.

=

The need to mix
happiness and grief

appears to be everywhere.

Endearment

Don't forget

how endearing light is
when it strikes something and appears
captivated,

the hanging crystal where, by passing through,
it can seem to stay,

and the webbed swags
of cypress, those graveclothes,
all a-twinkle.

—

This is what I need:
Goldilocks sun and a form
of mannered speech.

Split

There are pockets
of apocalypse.

Invaginations.

Don't wince.

I know you've always
appreciated correspondence—

the dormant stage
of contagion.

Some say truth
is a form
of parasitism:

"It is what it is."

Distal and proximal
halves split
down the midrib
of a leaf.

Acknowledgments

The author wants to thank the editors of the journals and anthologies in which these poems first appeared.

Journals: Academy of American Poets' Poem-a-Day, *American Poetry Review*, *Alligatorzine*, *The Believer*, *The Believer* online, *Big Other*, *Bomb*, *The Brooklyn Rail*, *Chicago Review*, *Common Knowledge*, *Conjunctions*, *Conjunctions* online, *Countertext*, *Dispatches*, *Golden Handcuffs Review*, *Goliad Review*, *Granta* online, *Guest*, *Hambone*, *Harper's*, *Interim*, *Jacket2*, *Lana Turner*, *The London Review of Books*, *The Los Angeles Review of Books*, *Mantis*, *The Nation*, *The New Yorker*, *The New York Review of Books*, *Paris Review*, *Pedestal*, *Peripheries*, *Plume*, *Poetry*, *Poetry Northwest*, *Women's Review of Books*.

Anthologies: *In the American Grain* (Europa Edizioni), *The Ekphrastic Writer: Creating Art-Influenced Poetry* (McFarland), *The Plume Anthology of Poetry 8* (Madhat Press), *Poems for the More-than-Human World* (Dispatches Editions), *Queenzenglish.mp3* (Roof Books), *Watch Your Head* (Coach House).

About the Author

Rae Armantrout, one of the founding members of the West Coast group of Language poets, stands apart from other Language poets in her lyrical voice and her commitment to the interior and the domestic. Born in Vallejo, California, Armantrout earned her B.A. at the University of California, Berkeley—where she studied with Denise Levertov—and her M.A. at San Francisco State University. The author of more than ten collections of poetry, Armantrout has also published a short memoir, *True* (1998). Her most recent collections include *Conjure* (2020); *Wobble* (2018), a finalist for the National Book Award; *Entanglements* (2017); *Partly: New and Selected Poems* (2016); and *Itself* (2015). *Versed* (2009) won the 2010 Pulitzer Prize in Poetry, a 2009 National Book Critics Circle Award, and was a finalist for the 2009 National Book Award. Her *Collected Prose* was published in 2007.